Where Did The

Sunrise Go?

Poetry by Rich Bergeron

Except for a few editorial corrections, some rearrangement, and the addition of one poem (Forever Road), the poetry in this publication is identical to the original release by Guild Press of Robbinsdale MN, published in 1984. The format has been changed to fit onto this paper size.

The cover photograph was taken by trojanbackoncommons at nl.wikipedia in 2004 near Driebergen, Netherlands. This photo was released to the public domain (worldwide) by its author. He grants anyone the right to use this work for any purpose without any conditions. Rich Bergeron found this photo at commons.wikimedia.org/wiki/file: sunriseinthemorning.JPG

ISBN: 978-989354301

Table of Contents

FORWARD: ABOUT RICH BERGERON

Once when I made a side trip into corporate America for my 9 to 5 (i.e. survival) I met a very unusual man over a computer terminal. A man whose mind and heart were full of Red Visions—not commie but Native American. Although he is White and I am Black, our common ground, through the medium of a 20th century computer, was a love of nature, a mutual recognition of the sacredness of life in all things and awe with the Great Mystery.

Rich is an unusual man of Catholic, working-class background. He grew up near urban industrial Chicagoland. He was one of the ones I was warned to watch out for when I "crossed the lines" of my Black southside Chicago neighborhood.

Here he is today working for a computer company, wearing Indian braids, married to a Jewish woman, and raising three sons, the eldest of whom is Black. Here he is toward the end of a very violent century, publishing a book of poetry in red, white, black, yellow, brown, blue and green; in fierceness and love; in flesh and spirit.

Here is a man who reaches out to embrace the world. He explores how human is connected to human — animal, vegetable and mineral too. In many ways the world is at peace within him. But I know he will not really be at peace until so many more of us find ways to go beyond the boundaries and make the world whole again.

Keep talkin' to us, Rich. Help us to hear, sense, touch and feel. Keep talkin', man…

Alemayehu[1]

---

[1] Louis Alemayehu is a highly respected teacher, poet and community organizer living in Minneapolis, MN, and a founding member of the jazz-poetry group named Ancestor Energy.

RESIDENTS OF HELL

After death there's only Heaven;
Hell is here on Earth:
When hungry children stand before us daily
        yet we turn our backs,
        knowing they shall die;
When charismatic leaders mouth their promises
        and we elect them once again
        knowing how they lie;
When self-directed interests
        rip our towns apart;
When selfish lovers
        laugh at others' hurting hearts;
When elders with a life's experience to give
        are forced to live
        their final days
        forgotten and alone;
When youthful dreams of hope and glory
        must claw their way along a gory path
        to non-existent future jobs and homes;
When hate, despair, hopelessness, and rage
        are forged on anvils
        made of crime, disease, neglect and pain;
When all of life's mythologies
        by fleeting new technologies
        are slain.
Then
After death
There's only Heaven.

NOMAD

Nomad wanders with a searching mind.
Lost amidst the mass of humankind,
He searches everywhere but cannot find
A place to anchor hopes and dreams,
Or even how to recognize
The meaning of his schemes.

Nomad,
The flotsam on life's raging river,
Grabs at anything that may deliver
Some release,
Some pity,
Love,
Surcease,
Some end to all the buffeting
And wild uncaring slow destruction
Of the searching soul.
Nomad,
Wanting to be whole,
Needing something to believe,
Meaningful ideas to conceive.

Nomad,
Everyman today is swept away
By people and events he doesn't recognize;
Everything in life is a surprise.
And never realizing where he is,
He cannot understand where he can go.

Nomad searches aimlessly for something...
Anything...
But never knowing where to find
His place amidst the mass of humankind,
Nomad wanders with a searching mind.

CALL OF THE TREE

Hey there, little boy,
Neighbor kids are coming.
Run around the buildings,
Escape into the woods.
Dance among the bushes,
Through the leaves I left
In autumns past.
Stop and chatter back
At sassy squirrels.
Call out to the sleeping owl.
Make believe that you're a wolf
And howl.
Trek across imagined wilderness
Of mountain hills and jungle gullies.
Hunt the vicious rhino cattle mooing softly
As you fight across the raging river creek.
Never mind
That you forgot to shed your shoes —
It's no news
That they can dry,
Perhaps before returning home.
Run until you find me.
Come on, climb me.
I will cradle you within my branches,
Let you meditate,
Contemplate the world that entrances.
But I'll never let the others find you.
I'll permit no interruptions
Of your dreams and fantasies.
Hey, there, little boy,
Neighbor kids are coming,
And I'm waiting here for you.

BABIES IN THE DIRT

See the baby sitting in the dirt?
The bloated stomach ever more grotesque
     and ribs protruding
         daily test the strength of baby skin.
It reaches out its hand
To help you understand
But never will you know a tenth
     of hunger's pain within.

See the baby sitting in the dirt.
You cannot tell the color of its skin
     because the haunted
        haunting eyes,
           too dry to shed a tear,
Will never let you see
Such triviality.
Instead, you're forced to concentrate
     upon the pain and fear.

See the baby sitting in the dirt.
Perhaps you'll halt and lend an ear
     to innocence that calls to you
        not knowing who to blame.
And listen carefully
To ageless misery
From cracked and bleeding lips that whisper
     "Hunger is my name."

These children,
even if they're far away,
        are yours.
All children are your future.
And so your fate your actions now decide.
Will you offer them a helping hand?
Or will you run away and hide?

What will you do?
You? …and you? …and you?
Will you save the children
        from their hurt?
Or will you turn your back again
        upon the babies in the dirt?

REMEMBERING

The small boy bows his head and cries
Without quite understanding why,
Remembering how his mother's hands
Would fly upon the keys to play Chopin;
Remembering, the stirring strands
Of Sousa from her phonograph,
Providing cadences for his marches
Round and round the table in the dining room.
He remembers how she loved the strains
Of the Beautiful Tennessee Waltz.
And he bows his head and cries.

The small boy bows his head and cries
And tries to keep the tears from being seen,
Remembering how his mother's soothing touch
Would fix the cuts and bruises from his falls,
How she persuaded swallows
        of some ghastly medicines.

He still feels her sympathetic hugs and kisses,
Hears the echo of her gentle laughter
When concerned about the daily fate of heroes on TV.
He remembers how she loved the strains
Of the Beautiful Tennessee Waltz.
And he bows his head and cries.

The small boy bows his head and cries,
The way his father did two years before
On that empty Christmas Eve.
That was the only time he'd seen his father weep
For Wife-and-Mother who was gone forever.
All the pain returns again,
On this assembly day at school.
The student band plays on, not realizing,
But the boy remembers
      how his mother loved the song—
The Beautiful Tennessee Waltz—
And he bows his head and cries.

ENGLISH CLASS

The poet-youth sits in his English class each day
And listens to the words the teacher has to say
About the greatest poets the language ever had,
Shakespeare, Byron, and Benet,
Milton, Sandburg, and Millay.
Deep inside the youth new feelings rise
From seeds of creativity these people planted.
He wrestles verses of his own
From deep inside himself,
And THINKS while he interprets
Vast arrays of literary wealth.

Then one day when called upon to have his say,
He explains the things he's come to understand.
He speaks from his experience,
Compares poetic style and tone,
Carefully explains the things he's learned
By writing verses of his own.
The teacher interrupts, insisting that he's wrong,
That what the poet's really saying in that song
Is something else again,
How could he so misinterpret...
And the teacher's voice goes on and no....
Finally the youth is able to respond.
He wonders why it's not all right to see
The meaning of these honored words in one's own
            way.
The teacher answers angrily:
"The meaning of these words is why I talk to you.
I've studied them for many years,
Not just a month or two.
If you do not buckle down—
Learn the things I say are true—
Then I'm afraid that I can only fail you."

Now the poet-youth resigns himself to memorize
The facts the English teacher has to say.
He never opens up the door again to be chastised...
And never writes another line of verse
Until his dying day.

STORM

There is no wind.
The sea is tame.
The ship is sailing smoothly on the glassy main.
The whole universe is quiet.
The vessel cruises silently beneath the stars
That twinkle, glitter, now appearing, disappearing,
Like the blazing heavens' avatars.
The ship continues slicing through the night
Accompanied by microflashes
As the plankton in the wake
Emancipate their tiny specks of light.

Suddenly wind begins to drive from peak to peak.
Seas become disorganized beneath agitated skies.
The tossing ship rolls and pitches wildly.
Constantly it seeks stability,
But slowly slips into troughs
Between raging waves.
Slams upon the surface of the briny deep,
Contesting anticipated endless sleep.

Waves reach out,
Smash with all their might,
Lash decks with fury
As worlds of air and sea and steel clash.
Frenzied waters crash
In attempts to drown the ship
That shudders, shivers, shakes,
As it tries to slip
From under tons of angry weight.
Slowly,
Inch by inch,
The vessel claws its way
Above liquid gray,

Returning to storm driven spray
To meet another trough,
Another raging wall.
Ship's antennas fall.
Lifelines rip away.
Paint's abraded by the salt.
But steel holds.

Exhausting hours later,
As the gale disappears,
The weary persevering crew
Presents a deep but silent sigh of thanks
To Neptune's retinue.

Slowly, oh so slowly,
The fatigued and battered ship
And all its men
Return to port to rest,
To be repaired,
To be prepared
To go to sea again.

SAN DIEGO GRAND PRIX

When ships are gone
The San Diego Grand Prix is begun.
When bars and nightclubs
Close at night
The race is lost or won.
I take my prize
And celebrate anew
The facts of life.
Rest easy, sailor,
While you're out at sea
I'll guard my prize
          your wife.

NEEDING

I stand here tall and proud and free,
Needing no one, no one needing me.
I have no burdens anywhere to weigh me down,
No wife, no kids, no childhood town
To settle me or woo me to unpack.
I have no cares or woes to hold me back.
I stand here tall and proud and free,
Needing no one, no one needing me.

I sometimes rendezvous with ladies of the night,
Knowing we will laugh and I'll be treated right
And be forgotten with the early light.
I don't look back when we put out to sea,
But dream of what tomorrow has in store for me.
I sail from port to port and back again
Aboard the ships of steel with other wooden men
To search among the noisy waterfront,
And never find a single truth amid my frantic hunt.

With each delight discovered in the search I taste
Another flavor of another place.
Though gutter-drunk from Jacksonville to Istanbul,
I follow hopes and dreams wherever they may pull,
But always do I find my cup is never full.
And still I stand here ever proud and free,
Refusing all connection with humanity.
By needing no one, no one needing me,
I find my solace when I'm thinking out at sea.

I stand alone surrounded by a hundred men,
Watch the playful porpoises again,
Offer up a prayer to sun's receding light,
Sail across the rolling swells of night
That sparkle with the agitated plankton bright

In answer to the twinkling stars above
That whisper of the universal secret's love.
Between the sea and sky I take my stance,
Make my first attempt at the eternal dance

I find I can't concern myself with where I go
As long as there is something new to know.
I'm driven, driven on to find where all this ends,
To grasp whatever life's adventure sends.
So I refuse to let myself have need
Of friends or anyone that may impede
My freedom to continue searching for my goal,
Find some kind of meaning in my soul,
Fill this emptiness and help to make me whole.

I stand here tall and proud and free,
Needing no one, no one needing me.
I have no burdens anywhere to weigh me down,
No wife, no kids, no childhood town
To settle me or woo me to unpack.
I have no cares or woes to hold me back.
I stand here tall and proud and free,
Needing no one, no one needing me.

GIFTS FROM VIET-NAM

Dick brought an end to the war in Viet-Nam.
John returned with a frazzled brain,
Joey with a needle in his arm.
Willie lost a leg somewhere in the jungles.
Matt is normal but divorced.
George jumps for cover every time a car backfires.
Jimmy's always looking for the booby-trap wires.
Andy keeps his eyes peeled for snakes there in the
        grass.
But Tricky Dick still has his head stuck up his ass.

COLLAGE IN WHITE

Now I lay me down to sleep.
I pray the Lord my soul to keep....

Jesus loves me, this I know
Because the Bible tells me so....

Eenie, meanie, miney, moe,
Catch a nigger by the toe.
If he hollers, let him go....

Daddy told the landlord yesterday
If he rents to jigaboos, we'll move away.

We learned all about Black folks in school, you see:
The slaves, George Washington Carver, and Booker
        T.

When Noah woke from drunken sleep
He cursed his son for all his days.
He said that Ham's offspring would be
Forever slaves to slaves.

I love pecans and walnuts and the rest,
But nigger-toes are really best.

Share that cigarette there in your hand,
But please don't nigger-lip it, man.

Blacks are great at sports and things.
Their music seems to give me wings.

A place for everything and everything in its place.
I guess the saying also goes for race.

Jesus taught us all God's wealth:
Love your neighbor as yourself.

I can't understand at all
Why those people aren't like us.
My grandfather stood up tall
And made it without all this fuss.

Feelings, knowledge I don't lack –
Some of my best friends are Black.

Come on son, I'll tuck you in
After prayers free you from sin.

Now I lay me down to sleep.
I pray the Lord my soul to keep...

Jesus loves me, this I know
Because the Bible tells me so....

SNOWFLAKES AND CINDERS

Why, O disillusioned people, do you dare
Depart from searching for the snowflake rare
To build a life with cinders, mud, and sand,
When those graceful crystals melt no longer on your
        hand?

INCENSE AND CANDLELIGHT

The sunny rays intrude
Upon the solitude
Of sleep
And prod me to awakening,
Urging me to rise.
The orb sings out And tries to brighten me
With light
That pours through opened window blinds
To flood the spot
On which I fell asleep last night.
As the haze of sleep recedes
There's brought to mind
The woman,
Incense, and the candlelight.

Upon remembering
I try once more to wrap myself
Into cocoons of sleep,
Intense security of night,
The incense and the candlelight.
But heaven won't return.

Before I even open up my eyes
I drift into the murky world
Of one-room attic lofts,
Stench of human animals,
Lumpy beds of straw,
Light of stubby candles
        Used as sparingly
        As possible.

This was my life until last night.
I met a little pixie
With her promises to stay with me
Throughout the night
And love by incense and the candlelight.

And with those words
The harsher lines of life like mine receded,
Driven deep into the night
By incense and the candlelight.

But now I'm all alone again.
I have to face a dreary solitude.
I force myself to open bleary eyes,
Find upon the shelf a candle freshly lit,
Realize the smell of incense
        That I thought remained from hours ago
           Is really so much more.

We gaze into each other's eyes,
Smile and kiss
And laugh a little bit
Because we realize
That we no longer need the night
For incense or for candlelight.

METAMORPHOSIS

I left my place of work.
I left my friends and came to you,
Discovered new horizons,
Found new depths of meaning in my life.
I found another family to be with.
When my year was up I'd changed so much
That I returned a stranger.

SPRING

Spring is just around the corner.
I can feel it!
It's raining all the time instead of snowing.
The birds are singing once again.
If you look just right at a silhouetted tree
Before a sometimes bright and bluish sky
The budding tips of branches can be seen.
Spring is just around the corner.
The clues are everywhere:
Little children playing in the mud
Instead of building structures made of snow;
The disappearing breed of tire chains;
Windbreakers that the people wear instead of coats.
The furry squirrels scampers out upon its hunt again,
Freezes at the sound of laughing squealing kids,
Then scurries up a tree.
The rapid rise of spring fever
Proves beyond a doubt
That spring is nearly here.
It's just around the corner!
I can feel it in my heart,
Which leaps and bounds in bright anticipation
Of the times when we can walk along the cliffs again,
Or stroll across the clover fields
Where we can pick the dandelions that we use to see
        if butter still will show beneath our chins.
I'll pick a flower for your hair
And from another
I will hand you, one by one,
Those velvet soft and fragrant petals
Which forever end the chant with "Yes, she loves
        me."

Spring is just around the corner.
Can't you feel it?
I sure can!

THE TOUCH

On we go
each alone
marching to our different drums
stepping off
our ticks in time
unsynchronized
until
by accident
we touch
for just
a moment
       then on we go
       each alone
       marching to our different drums
       that take us on our ways
but who can say
we're unchanged
through our remaining days?

CHANGING

I got so angry —
She said she loved me
       Just the way I was —
Then she tried to change me.
God! I got so angry.

Now I am so thankful.
She said she loved me
       Then helped me change
Become more open
       Loving
       And responsible —
And still me!

I get to thinking
How good her nagging was for me
Even though
I didn't like it then.
So now I'd rather stay,
      Change a little more,
Than leave —
And have to do it all again.

EDEN'S PATH

The charming back road that I follow
Twists and turns through gentle hills
To finally rest beside the sparkling sea.
Softly sighing breeze's sounds
Caress the foliage strewn around
This Island Paradise.
The pathway, lined with coral walls,
Meanders near a waterfall
That pirouettes in nature's dance.
Verdant ivy leaps
To kiss a footbridge fast asleep.
This gem, Bermuda,
Brilliantly reflects the golden rays
of sunny peace that pierce my heart.
Ever present coastal songs
That ride the currents of the air
Mingle with the cattle's prayer,
Call to everyone:

"Oh, people, come!
Relax!
Unwind!
Behold my splendor!"

Then I find a blighted cedar tree,
A blemish on the face of purity,
Reminding me that every year
We still destroy
Such Edens
In our satanic race
As we shatter every trace
of Mother Nature's grace.

I hear another whisper in the breeze
That pleads:
"Are you sufficiently awake
To go back home
And there
Repair the hell you've helped to make?"

WORDS

While walking through the park
      the other day
I saw a man
      resplendent in his
            scraggly hair
            tangled mustache
            rough unshaven face
            wrinkled clothes
            pen and pad of paper.
He seemed oblivious to all the world about him
      as he sat upon the grass
            etching thoughts upon the pad
      and then
      within the blinking of an eye
      his pen of fire
      had purged the words.
He ripped apart the soiled page
      crumpled it
      stuffed it deep into his pocket
      as he gazed about himself.
My eyes met his
      but then I turned my gaze away
      because it seemed that he could see
      into the very depths of me.

Then I heard a clicking noise.
I chanced
      a glance again
      and saw the man
      now holding peanuts in his hand:
            a peaceful handout to a furry ball of
      gray.

He chattered then again.
Perhaps he thought he was a squirrel too.

And perhaps he was because
        the animal came over to the outstretched hand
        picked up a nut and ate,
        then made another choice again
            and then again
            until the hand was bare
            but still outstretched
            it seemed for something
            to be given in return.

The poet's eyes were closed
        as if he dreamed of other days
        when words came easily.

He fished into his pocket
        and retrieved the pad and pen.
And then
        he jotted down a couple lines
            scrutinized them ...
            shook his head ...
            made a change ...
            scratched it out ...
            began again ....
After long and painful minutes
He stuffed the paper back into his pocket
        which already he had filled
        with his discarded scraps
And looking at the setting sun
        he shook his head
        as if he doubted that the words
            had ever really come
            as easily as he remembered them.

Thenstanding with a movement brusque
        he walked into the dusk.

MARK OF CAIN

The mark of Cain
surrounds you
Ur-Shalom,
       Ur-Salaam,
              Jerusalem,
City of Peace.
Your sons and daughters stand
beside barbed-wire barricades,
artillery,
and fields of deadly mines.
All your Semitic sons and daughters,
Jew and Arab,
separate each other from each other,
splash their bloody marks
upon themselves,
while laying waste the no-man's land ...
brother killing brother ...
sister hating sister ...
father damning father ...
mother praying
       mother ...
              praying ....
The time is yet to come
oh, Ur-Salaam,
       Ur-Shalom,
you city peaceful in name only,
when your children will cleanse
the Mark of Cain
each from the other's brow.

FINAL FLOWER

I gaze upon the dry and windy plain,
The specter of a planet writhing in its pain.
Foreign mountains worn to dust
Sweep high into the air,
Pull the clouds from perches in the sky,
Reach out to hide the shining sun,

Swoop to cover up the single flower standing there –
That final flower rooted in the earth
Which gave it birth.
No longer living
Are the plains that used to roll forever
In the glory of the prairie grass.
In the silent mid-day dusk,
So dark that I cannot even see my hand,
The final flower of the land
Droops its head
And dies
There
Next to the final tear I shed.

VISIT TO A MOUNTAINTOP

I used to smile ...
Maybe even laugh a bit ...
Joke around ...
Then retreat back into darkness,
Hiding in the shadows,
The gloom ...
The loneliness ...
The hell ....

Until you took me to a mountaintop
And spent a while up there with me
Where we could hold each other's hands
Gaze upon the world, laugh, sing
Hold each other as the bells forever ring
To the tone of touching lips and sighing eyes.

But then we had to part
And follow separate paths for a while.
All I do is dream away
Every lonely night and day
Wipe away a tear ...
Dream of bells that ring ...
Dream of touching lips ...
Dream of sighing eyes ...
Dream of having you nearby ...
Dream of you ...
Dream ....

SUNSHINE FRIENDS

Dark and dreary
Drizzly cold and rainy days
Surround me now
And fill my heart with longing
For the friends I left behind
When having to depart.

I miss you and your light,
My sunshine friends,
Flashing warmth with every smile.
It's so hard to fill the void
By being with you
Only once a week
For just a little while.

MIND DIET

Bodies slim and sleek
Result from all the diet books
That sell so very well,
While minds grow fat and lazy.
Thinking steadily becomes more hazy
Until limp and useless brains
Sag like paunches
Blocking sight of mindless eyes
That never see a need for mental exercise,
And owners boast of greatness
Based on flabby size alone.
But where's the mental muscle tone?
Somewhere, soon,
We have to find
A special diet
For the mind.

SLEEP IN PEACE

To my wife Barbara, and our unborn son, Ari, that summer in
Red Wing, Minnesota, 1970.

Sleep in peace and take your rest.
I'll hold you tightly to my breast,
Protect you with my might,
Watch over unborn light.
       Will he stand up straight and tall?
       Will he look like you or me?
       Will she grow to womanhood
       Standing tall and free?
It's up to us, you know,
To guide him as he grows,
To make her strong,
To be the best.
       So sleep in peace
       And take your rest.
       For soon the time will come
       To bring the newest to the nest.

BIGOTRY

I don't know who you are:
Muslim
Christian
Buddhist
Hindu
Jew.
Neither do I care.
But there's one thing you must remember
As peoples rise and fall:
God teaches us to love,
And bigotry has got to be
The greatest sin of all.

GOING HOME

Going home,
Going home to valleys green
And rolling hills of grass and trees,
Whose blades and branches
Dance before the gently blowing breeze.
Going home at last.

Departing years ago with anger in my heart
I searched for love and life
But had to reach from hell
For anchor in the storm.
Nothing there was warm,
Just coldly raging self and strife.
I thought that only loneliness
Could fight the mirror image,
Wrestle angels' wings in downward flight,
Ever downward from the light,
Until the gutter slapped me in the face.
Then the race within myself was over.
Going home.

But anger fills my heart no more.
It's been replaced by love and life,
A newfound wife,
Another anchor in the storm.

Up we climb together
Through the valleys green
And rolling hills of grass and trees,
Whose blades and branches
Dance before the gently blowing breeze.

Going home at last.

IMAGES OF DAD

To all fathers who believe that parenting comes naturally.

The little boy is growing up
With everything his family has.
He's learning all the good and bad,
Including images of Dad.

Always he must be hard-working,
Truthful, and "a man,"
Just follow blindly all the dictates,
Allowances, and bans.

The boy lives in a double-bind
That gives him so much pain.
His Father shouts: "You have a brain!
Why don't you ever use it?
It's a gift of God and a sin if you abuse it."
But every time he tries to learn alone,
To do a few things on his own, he gets chastised
With anger bordering upon the absolutely mad.
And deep inside the boy solidifies his images of Dad.

Father amplifies the stresses
And unconsciously impresses
On the boy in every way he can
The modern contradiction
Of the term "a gentle man."

The youth is learning lessons well,
Suppressing things he wants to tell,
Which Father will not hear, anyway.
He learns to breathe the atmosphere
Of anger, ranting, raving,
Spanking, violence, incredible behaving.
No one ever notices the boy is sad.
No one ever sees the vicious images of Dad.

There's never time for hunting,
Fishing, or a baseball game,
For Father's tired or busy
Or he has some other reason –
Perhaps another season ....
And that is that
Because the boy can never question
Any word that Father says.
And there is nothing anyone can add
To help the boy who's locked
Into the images of Dad.

Now the boy is grown
With children of his own –
Normal, healthy sons
Running merrily
Among the scattered toys
And making playful noise
Which irritates the man.
He lets his anger,
Raging and intense,
Override his common sense.
He slaps and spanks
And shouts at boys
Who learn,
In turn,
To keep their faces blank.

He lays the first foundations,
And there's nothing else to add.
Unconsciously he guarantees that all his sons
Will promulgate his images of Dad.

HAIR

I've come to the conclusion
That the world
So disillusioned
Puts a great amount of value on my hair
'Cause when I'm out of work
Each employer,
Through some quirk,
Requires that I see a barber to work there.
Then when I desire to gey more pay
The Boss insists
here's just one way:
All I have to do is cut my hair —
To there.

MALCOLM X

Malcolm,
Through your angry words
There shines a sense
Of Justice

I seek justice, too.

You once said
You'd shake the hand
Of any human being.

I wish that you were still around
So you might take the time
To see
If I qualify.

UNSUNG HERO

The booming banging hellish roar of battle
Smothers his tormented screams
As crimson liquid oozes
Through the soldiers hands
So tightly clenched to dampen out the pain.
      The lonely silent tears that flow away
      From young and dying dreams
      To mingle salt with scarlet
      Alters not the drying hue of life's receding
      stream.
The numbing throb of
Stomach-ache
Contractions
Rumbles out
Echoes on
Joins in concert
With the growing pool of blood
To sing a fatal song.
      And all the while
      The sap of life
      Drip
      Dribbles silently
      Through whitened
      Stiffened
      Hands
      Ignoring armaments
      Of sedatives and sutures,
      Pills and gauze, and tape in cans.
When lifeless eyelids finally close
The corpsman's blood has flowed
To hide the color of the cross of red
Upon his fallen helmet band.

FORGIVE ME

Forgive me please
For leaving you alone.
I didn't know where I was going –
I had to find myself along the way.
And though I needed help,
I didn't recognize the hand you offered;
I never knew how I could help you in return.

Forgive me, friends,
For leaving when I did,
For luring you to give yourselves,
Your homes, your hearts, your time and services.
You held a mirror up for me.
You guided me to recognize so many faults
And still remained a friend when I had gone.
I didn't recognize the hand you offered;
I never knew how I could help you in return.

Forgive me, ladies,
For stealing from your love,
Accepting offers I could not refuse.
I used your shoulders then to cry upon,
And took the bodies that you gave me,
Wrapping your dependence all around myself
To give my soul another hiding place.
I didn't recognize the hand you offered;
I never knew how I could help you in return.

Forgive me, father,
Aunts and uncles, too.
I didn't know what family was back then
And had to learn its meaning once again.
You always gave your understanding, opened up your
           arms and hearts to me.
Now that you are gone from life on Earth
I finally recognize the hand you offered.
Too late, I cannot thank you for your love.

Forgive me please
For leaving you alone.
I didn't know where I was going –
I had to find myself along the way.
And though I needed help,
I didn't recognize the hand you offered;
I never knew how I could help you in return.

VOICES

The Voice
In the dream
Didn't sound bad
Didn't sound mean,
Instead,
Just a little bit sad
When it said:
"Why do we have
Only nothing
To say
Any more?"

TROPIC ZONES

For Bruce Henry, when he was the lead vocalist of the band,
        Tropic Zone.

Seven men upon the stage
Entrance
The people in the audience.
They sing and dance
And pilot us
Into a hundred other worlds.
Seven men manipulate our souls,
Weaving threads of music
In and out to make us whole.
And then,
They change their tempo,
Add a flute and castanets
To take us on a tour
Of sunny Spain
Or bright Brazil,
Or anywhere they wish to go.
The seven men can play the stars
Reflecting once again
From midnight velvet
Shining through our eyes.
And nevermore
Will we return to simple homes
Because the seven men
Have taken us

To Tropic Zones.

COMMUNION

It's beautiful outside.
Lightning swords set fire to the night.
Thunder rumbles just beyond
The sound of pitter-patting rain.
      I was going to put some music on.
      I'm glad I didn't do it now.

Vivid splashing bluish light
Permits the view of outside being washed.
I wonder, How ...
How can I know what's going on inside?
      I get the feeling,
      When the lightning cries,
      That Voices try to speak to me again.
      I wonder what's it all about.

I feel all washed and clean inside again,
So different from the past few ... days?
How long's it been since we communed?
"Go on," the Voice enticed
So many months ago.
Where have I gone since then?
How much more is yet to know?
And where is there to go?
      Who knows?

I'll go wherever I will go,
Dream my dreams,
Do the things I've got to do.
I'll live and grow.
      I feel all washed and clean inside again.
      I get the feeling,
      When the lightning cries,
      That Voices try to speak to me again ....

TOUCHING

I saw a young Black poet
As he read his work one night.
He walked around the room
And touched the other Blacks
So gently,
Silently,
Upon the shoulder
As he read.
I didn't understand
His touching.

So now you may be asking
Why this white-skinned dude
Has come among you,
Passing through the crowd
And touching too
When even he admits
He didn't understand.

But as the last few months have passed
I've felt a touching of my own.
A seed within my soul has grown.

You've seen the spider
Weave her thread
So delicate
Intricate;
She touches point to point
A couple of things
With all her silken strings.

But how does that relate
To why I'm touching you?

I see all our people in a web
With tiny threads connecting
Each one to the others.
Call it spirit, call it soul,
Or maybe it is just a being whole.
All of us participate in life together
And it doesn't even matter whether
We desire it or not –
That web of life is there,
And touching.

That young poet
Only touched the other Blacks.
But now I'm touching all of you –
Not because you're Black or Yellow, Red or White.
Now I understand why he was touching.
I'm tying each of us to every other,
For I recognize our sharing of the same Earth Mother
And the Father Sun who gives to all of us his light,
Touching us to show us what is right.

We're in this life together,
Touching,
Reaching out for help
And comfort
From another human being,
And it doesn't make a bit of difference
What your color is outside.
We're touching
All our hearts and hopes and dreams.
Everything important
With a universal theme
Is touching
In the web together

Each and every one of us
Is grasping,
Clutching,
Reaching out for mutual support.

TOWER BABBLE

People gather round
To make their talking sounds,
Screaming at each other,
Yelling,
Shouting down,
Until he crowded rabble
Represents the Tower Babble.

Spire on spire,
Growing ever higher,
Tumble when you will.
Screeching throats are getting drier.
Soon they'll all be still.

Millions of distorted faces
Gather from a thousand places,
Mouth their hidden-meaning
Symbols noisily,
While spiteful hating rabble
Keep on building Tower Babble.

Those abhorring soldier toys
Are drowned within the sea of noise,
As missiles fly
And warheads die.
So very few remain,
None of all the rabble
Representing Tower Babble.

Spire on spire,
Growing ever higher,
Tumble in the end.
Those who live on through the fire
Finally comprehend.

ALONE WITH YOU AGAIN

Work is over.
Supper, too.
The dishes done
Or waiting in the sink
To greet the morning sun.

Now's the time we can relax —
Write or read,
Or lose ourselves
To TV's sights and sounds,
Talk about
      Today's events,
      Tomorrow's hopes and dreams,
      Or yesterday's mistaken schemes,
Or simply rest a weary head.

All the kids
Have finally gone to bed.

And whether we sit hand in hand
Or do our different things
There in the den,
I'm glad to be alone
With you again.

SEEDS

Men and women shake the crowd
In silence through the lake of sound
While planting patient seeds of light.
Boredom inundates your world
Through house and car,
Eight hours of work,
And empty glasses at the bar.
Within your aggravation,
Consternation,
Restless agitation,
Flower children sow the seeds of discontent
To grow within the night.

Men and women wake the crowd
While searching through the lake of sound.
The seedlings start to sprout
From underneath the ground
And quietly begin to shout:
"Your house and car, though very nice,
Your unproductive job
And church of ice,
Corrode the meaning of your life
And help to plant the seeds of search."

Men and women shake the world,
Cut their care,
Lay aside their bells and beads,
Leave the isolation
Of idealist communities,
Go to college,
Get a job.
They find new pathways in the night,
Growing, teaching, finally reaching
Outward with their light.

Within your aggravation,
Consternation,
Restless agitation,
Tender plants are grown
From seeds of learning
Which are sown.

Men and women shake the crowd
And make their presence known.
The flowers of their silent sound
From underneath the ground
Begin to bloom.
Dawn arrives.
In the light
The flower children's blossoms rise up high
To shout:
"The house and car are nice to own,
But fruit as yet untaken
Grows to show a way of life
From seeds that we awaken."

RETREAT

At the religious retreat
I hear so many good and beautiful words
My spirit is uplifted.
I take my many notes
With a felt tip pen,
And then the raindrops
Wash them all away –
I'm left with only those things
Living in my heart.
I'm still richer
Than I was before I came.

WHERE DID THE SUNRISE GO?

I hear the pounding of the Army's boots
Breaking through the silence of the night
As the flower of our youth is sent away to war
  To war ...
To deadly, senseless war,
While mothers, wives, and lovers
Shed their useless tears
For those who will return
From battles they are proud to fight,
Or so the leaders say.
  I wander through the land
  In search of things no longer there
  To ask the people
  Of the mountains and the seashore sand.
  But no one seems to know.
  Where did the sunrise go?

I hear the footsteps of the rioters
Screaming in the silence of the night,
As the flower of our youth
Demands the promised freedom,
  Freedom ...
That misty myth called freedom.
My children wake and cry
Their tears of innocence
And ask why we've not given them
Those freedoms which we have to give.
And silence must I keep.
  I wander through the land
  In search of things no longer here
  To ask the people of the bayou, plains, and
  lakes.
  But no one seems to know.
  Where did the sunrise go?

I see the empty shadows in the church
Where no one worships any more
On any day or night,
For the flower of our youth
Was sent away for truth,
      Truth ...
The Holy Grail, truth,
Which now is gone forever.
The ancient God is dead, Buried by hypocrisy,
For peace and love are nowhere taught
Sincerely any more.
      I wander through the land
      In search of things no longer here
      To ask the people of the rivers
      and the forest land.
      But no one seems to know.
      Where did the sunrise go?

Once upon a time we had a pride to show
Breaking through the silence of the night.
But now the flower of our youth
Has nothing to believe,
      Believe ...
What is there to believe?
Our star has set some time ago
And no one seems to know
Where ancient spirit's gone.
Betrayed by those before us,
Darkness bathes our way.
      I wander through the land
      In search of things no longer here
      To ask the people of the valley and the desert
      sand.
      But no one seems to know.
      Where did the sunrise go?

GLOBAL PRAYER

In Australia's pretty Perth,
In Moscow, Glasgow, Tripoli,
Singapore, Bangalore, and sunny Napoli,
People kneel and beg.

In London, Lisbon, Dublin, Durban,
In Bombay and Yaoundé
Split Berlin and Kalinin,
People wait and hope.

From Rio, Cairo, Nairobi,
Ottawa, Massawa, gay Paree,
New York state and far Sydney,
Farms and jungles near Quang Tri,
You can hear the cries.

From mountain folk in Bogota,
The starving young of Biafra,
The multitudes of Red Canton,
And farther south, those in Saigon,
Voices pray without surcease
For justice, honesty, and peace.

SHOCK

Shock!

See the Pilgrim Fathers
Silently surround the Pequot village
In the night before the dawn.
See them hold their guns
A mere six inches from the ground
And pull the triggers,
Shooting sleeping people.
Then they scalp the women,
Men and children that they mock.

See the ship that overflows
With human cargo,
Black-skinned people
Who survived the voyage.
Men and women with their children,
Families
Are torn apart

And sold from on the block.
See the Chinese coolie
Working in the broiling sun,
Pounding spikes to hold the rails
Of the greatest country's glory roads
For trains to carry all the cargo
Inland from the dock.

See the Army's soldiers
Taking blankets from
The smallpox dead and dying,
Pass them on to freezing Native people
With their children crying,
Wipe them out like sheep
For slaughter by the flock.

See the children
In the West Virginia coal mines
And the textiles mills of Massachusetts.
Bloody coughs and mangled fingers
Glorify the god of profit,
While the foremen keep the children
Working eighteen hours a day until they drop.

See the Colorado volunteers come charging
Down upon the enemy who flies a flag of white,
Use the Cheyenne toddlers for their target practice,
Slash the pregnant mothers with their sabers,
Scalp the private parts,
While laughing at the tears that fall upon the
U.S. flag the chief has draped around himself
While crying, "Friends! We're friends!"
Until he drops.

See the hanging judge
Roy Bean at work,
Sitting on his porch
And hearing all the accusations,
Passing down his sentences of death.
It makes no difference
What the hundred Mexicans have done,
Or whether they are even guilty,
For the lawman's only interest
Lies in ridding Texas of the Spanish-speaking lot.

See the white folks of Chicago
Laugh and dance in glee
To see the Negro worker's child
Drowning at the public beach.
And not a single helping hand is offered.
Then, when Black folks show their anger,
All Chicago's best unleash their savagery
And kill a hundred more
While putting down the riots
Block by block.

See the Japanese who bought your system,
Worked like you and grew successful,
Too successful.
See, third generation citizens
Are put behind the barbed-wire fences,
Guarded in the concentration camps,
No longer owning homes and shops.

Shock!

Wake up, America!
And see the glory of the nation
Built upon the blood of millions who have lived,
And worked,
And loved,
And died
To build this country,
Willingly or not.

Shock!

ONE WAY STREET

It amazes me the people that I meet
Upon the one-way street.
You'd think the dark-skinned people,
So mistreated for so long,
Would have much more to lose
By letting all their feelings show.
But still, when white folks go to them,
They open up their homes and hearts
And let their depths of loving flow.
But if the dark-skinned people go the other way,
No matter how sincere and warm,
Expecting friendship in return,
The traffic cop is there to censure
And enforce the social norms.
It amazes me the people that I meet
Upon this country's one-way social street.

DON'T KNOW

Don't know where I'm goin'.
Don't know where I've been.
Don't know what I'm doin'.
Not even where or when.
Don't know why I'm here or there
Or why I never win.
Don't know who to turn to,
So, Brother, pass the gin.

MINSTREL

The day the wandering minstrel first arrived
He asked us if we'd spare a little time
To listen to him sing of love and other things,
Like peace for humankind.

. We laughed and jeered,
For he was old, bent over by his age,
Hardly capable of holding up his lute.
But as he sat upon the grass,
Snuggled close the body of his instrument,
His fingers flew,
Caressing softly all the strings at once.
We could see a master of his art was he.

Singing just a couple haunting songs
With softened voice he overcame
Our shouts and laughter,
So lovingly he plied his trade,
Soothing us who lived in hate,
And challenged:
:Listen to me if you dare,
If you think you care,
If you have the courage to be honest with yourself."

He said he'd sung when he was young,
Long before the war.
But no one listened to him then.
He shed a tear and said just loud enough to hear:

"And now your cities carry hidden death,
Forbidding you to live the way you did before,
Forcing you to carry on in nature's way.
You wish to know eternal spring,
But if you did, then you would kill it too,
For do you not destroy all else you know
That gives you life and love?
But spring flows into summer,
      autumn winds to snow,
These cannot be controlled.
But some day you will find your way –
And then you'll know yourself to be
      the spring of life."

He lived with us for just a couple months,
Taught us how to live in happiness.
Every night around the fire
We'd lounge and listen to him sing.
And when he knew he'd sung enough
He left our tents
And wandered on to others
That were filled with hate as we had been.

The day he left
He asked of us
To disavow hypocrisy,
To live the brotherhood
To which we mouthed our words.
He called us near,
Said just loud enough for us to hear:
"Learn to give of all you have.
Betray your Christmas
Which requires you to give but once a year.
But give instead the whole year through,
Willingly,
Each day anew,
And you shall live in peace.

Then he turned

To make his way
Across horizons
Where his songs were needed more.
And as he wound his way along the path
We thought we heard him sing:
"You listened to my songs
Of truth,
Love,
Peace for humankind.
You dared to care,
To be honest with yourself –
You shall live in peace."

HARLEQUIN

In honor of Michel Langinieux, a real Harlequin

I am Harlequin.
I know who I am inside,
And have no need to ask.
I am Harlequin,
A clown behind a mask.

I see each of you out there
With masks upon your face
Rushing madly round and round
And staying in your place!

Jump and dance and mimic, too,
But never shed a tear.
Dare not let emotions show
For then you might be queer!

I am Harlequin.
I know who I am inside,
And have no need to ask.
I am Harlequin,
A clown behind a mask.

Point your finger everywhere
At him and her and that.
Only time you point to you
Is when you don your hat!

You can say what others are
The black and brown and red.
Why then can you not decide
What's really in your head?

I am Harlequin.
I know who I am inside,
And have no need to ask.
I am Harlequin,
A clown behind a mask.

View another, one to one.
Now, are you face to face?
Might there really be but one
That's sharing common space?

Each of you perceives yourself
And that is all you care.
Can you really understand
The feelings that you share?

I am Harlequin.
I know who I am inside,
And have no need to ask.
I am Harlequin,
A clown behind a mask.

Point to you and think a while
On what you're told you are.
If that's all that you can be
You won't go very far!

Flee from life until you meet
The death mask of your fate.
Keep on running 'til you die.
You'll stop when it's too late!

I am Harlequin.
I know who I am inside,
And have no need to ask.
I am Harlequin,
A clown behind a mask.

I am Harlequin.
I'm one you cannot rule.
I'm the Harlequin,
But really, Who's the fool?

SPECTRE

The days I died from bullets and disease
I promised I would haunt your dreams.
I rise from many graves
To stand beside your beds at night,
To touch your hearts,
To slowly change your nightmares
Into visions of a future Eden.
I'm all that's left of ancient peoples,
Spectre of a paradise encased in concrete,
Locked in timeclocks,
Crucified by loving neighbors,
Honored by children spitting on extended families
Spread from coast to coast.
I keep my promise:
Here I am, standing ever silently beside you
Watching ... Watching ...
              Watching ... Watching ....

TO INFINITY

The city stands alone,
Silent in the murky gloom.
Its empty streets.
Are cluttered by the scattered ruined
Buildings' fingers
Reaching futily to touch the sky.
And even though
No contact can be made,
The scarred and blackened city's bones
Extend themselves,
Reach out to infinity.

What is left for me to do
Now that my world exists no more,
Except return myself,
Try to find the few remaining
Quiet fields,
Virgin woods,
The people that survived,
Try again to reach out to infinity?

The city stands alone,
Deadly in the murky gloom,
It's empty air
Devoid of all the life we knew:
The sparrows,
Thrushes,
Hawks and doves,
All went the way
The people went,
Their bony dust
Was washed away

By poisoned rain
That fell down through contaminated night
Of glowing neutrons,
Unseen micro-organisms,
And the gas of silent sleep
That reaches out to infinity.

The city stands alone,
Crying in the murky gloom.
Another structure crumbles,
Topples, smashes to the ground,
None remain to hear the sound
Of mankind's graveyard
Sleeping, weeping, all alone,
For no one's there to place a flower on the grave.
And wild flowers grow no more
From black and glassy shores
That reach out to infinity.

What is left for me to do
But travel on, try to live some kind of life
Upon a clean and sparkling riverbank.
If one could just be found
That reaches to infinity?

FOREVER ROAD

A road goes on forever,
No beginning and no end,
Forever 'round and 'round,
Turning back upon itself
So gradually
You never realize it's doing so.
That road goes on forever
In your mind.

On the road that goes forever
You travel happy and content,
Singing as you march by vistas
Seen a hundred times before,
       Again and yet again,
       Like familiar favorite paintings.
On you go
Ignoring all the side roads –
       The unpaved,
       Dusty,
       Leading-to-unknown-places side roads –
You ignore them,
Continue on in comfort,
On the road that goes forever,
'Round and 'round ...
'Round and 'round ...
'Round and 'round ...

THE LOCAL DAILY DOG AND PONY SHOW

Pull that mask across your face.
Straighten out your coat and tie.
Smile for everyone at work
And ooze enthusiasm as you tell them why
You're glad to be there once again.

Make a perfect jump through every hoop.
Run around your circle
Dancing, prancing, proud to do your tricks.
Do them right
So all the managers can have their kicks
And beam at you with pride.

Glow when you get patted gently on the head.
The show continues,
Everyone performing flawlessly
And acting out their parts.
But you know that even bosses know
What it's really all about
When they welcome your return
To the local daily dog and pony show.

WATCH THE CHILDREN GROW

Watch the children grow.
Watch them carefully.
Teach them what you know
But give them room
To bloom.
Be there when they need you
While you let them stand alone.
When you watch the children grow.

BUGGY

See my old junk heap car,
My "buggy."
Its body is so rusted out
That much of it simply isn't there.
The heater doesn't work.
Neither do half the windows.
And the engine –
That's why I call it "buggy,'
'Cause there's just a single horse
Left underneath the hood.

RESIDENT OF HELL'S RESPITE

I said that Hell is here on Earth
And nothing's changed my mind.

I try to feed the hungry children,
     disavow the politicians' lies,
     learn of others' needs and empathize,
     respect my elders and children's dreams ...

And even though I do the best I can
That Hell still rages through the land.

So what is there
     that makes it worth me staying here?
What keeps me going
     through the Hell my predecessors made?
Why don't I simply quit – suicide –
     get it over with?

I'll tell you why.

I know respite from shattered hopes and dreams.
I know what Heaven's like.
For when she holds me in her arms,
     and soothes my burning fevers
          with her soft caress,
     when she melts away my fears and pains
          with one sweet kiss,
     when she bares my very soul
          with her penetrating eyes
She stokes the fires of love
That make this Hell on Earth
     a thing that I'll survive.

I said that Hell is here on Earth –
And nothing's changed my mind.
But now I have the strength
to keep on trying to smother flames
         of ignorance, hunger, hatred, pain, and lies
For I've already tasted Paradise.

Biography of the Author

Rich Bergeron, a Dakota Sioux by adoption, is married to Barbara Rothman Bergeron, who is Jewish. Their oldest son is Black and Cherokee. Their younger sons are Eastern European and French-German-Scottish; their family is a mini-United Nations.

Rich worked as a technical educator for many years, but lived for his history and cultural studies. Then he got his dream job designing social studies software for MECC (Minnesota Educational Computing Corporation / The Learning Company). After his most recent formal employment, he volunteered for two years with AmeriCorps and another year with VISTA. Now he spends his time teaching with Minneapolis Community Education and writing.

His poetry has also been published in a number of Guild Press anthologies. He has written other items that were published in numerous media, including the Internet; "Three Acadian Generations" is an example of the latter. He is presently working on his first novel, *Ripple Effect*. His intense interest in social, cultural and racial issues is reflected in this, his first book of poems—*WHERE DID THE SUNRISE GO?*

www.ingramcontent.com/pod-product-compliance
Lightning Source LLC
Chambersburg PA
CBHW060713030426
42337CB00017B/2851